The Self-Styled No-Child

4-23-19

The Self-Styled No-Child

Cody Walker

Cody W...

For Audrey, on her very
last day as an undergrad!
Here's to the many adventures
ahead —

With every good wish,

Cody

WAYWISER

First published in 2016 by

THE WAYWISER PRESS

Christmas Cottage, Church Enstone, Chipping Norton, Oxon OX7 4NN, UK
P.O. Box 6205, Baltimore, MD 21206, USA
http://waywiser-press.com

Editor-in-Chief
Philip Hoy

Senior American Editor
Joseph Harrison

Associate Editors
Dora Malech | Eric McHenry | V. Penelope Pelizzon | Clive Watkins
Greg Williamson | Matthew Yorke

A CIP catalogue record for this book is available from the British Library

·

ISBN 978-1-904130-70-3

Printed and bound by
T. J. International Ltd., Padstow, Cornwall, PL28 8RW

For my parents, Alison and Bright

ACKNOWLEDGMENTS

My thanks to the editors of the following journals in which these poems first appeared, sometimes in earlier versions:

Birmingham Poetry Review: three sections from "Small Suite" ("Third Trimester," "Origin Song," "In Two Hundred Years")

Cellpoems: a section from "Three, Briefly" ("At a Tennis Court, at Amherst College, Near the Frost Library")

The Common: "Cradle Song"

Crab Creek Review: "Deuteronomy, Continued"

The Equalizer: "Haiku," "The Jerk Speaks," "A Long Time Ago, in Italy," "Absolut Power Corrupts Absolut-ly"

Gigantic: "Appetite"

Light Quarterly: "Upward Mobility," "Mid-January"

Mad Hatters' Review: "Un-jokes," "Poem with an Epigraph from *Edward Lear, King of Nonsense,* a Biography for Young People," "All the Splendid Babies"

Mare Nostrum: "Petronius"

Matter: "2011-2012: A Romnibus" (without the second of the two limericks: "With six weeks to go, Barry blinks"), "Aurora Black-out"

The Monarch Review: "Autobiography," "Newtown Carol"

Okey-Panky: "OK, a Dude's Dead, But You Can Go"

Poetry Northwest: "The Art of Poetry," "Trades I Would Make," "This Is the Neighbor Kid Who Killed the Cat," "Quatrains," "When Addison Strode the Earth," "Mind of Winter," "Disconsolation," "A Mad Gardener's Half Dozen," "News That Stays News," "Days, Months, Years"

Qualm: "Seasonalia," a section from "Small Suite" ("Staggering Backwards"), "We Hated Our Lives," a section from "Three, Briefly" ("Amy Clampitt, Wary Huntress"), "Most Beautiful and Most Wonderful"

Salon: a section from "2011-2012: A Romnibus" (the second of the two limericks)

The Seattle Review: "A Skeleton Walks Into a Bar"

Spillway: "This Again"

Tampa Review: "The Self-Styled No-Child"
Unsplendid: "What I Want"
The Yale Review: "Lenox, Early Spring"

"The Art of Poetry," "Seasonalia," and "The Self-Styled No-Child"
    were reprinted in *Bear River Review 2013*.
"Cradle Song" was reprinted in *Uncommon Core: Contemporary
    Poems for Learning and Living* and *Bear River Review 2014*.
"Mind of Winter" was reprinted in *Peninsula Poets*.
"Trades I Would Make" was reprinted in *The Best American Poetry
    2015*.

I'm grateful to the Richard Hugo House, the Amy Clampitt Fund,
the Helen Riaboff Whiteley Center, and the Sewanee Writers' Con-
ference for residency and fellowship assistance. And I'm particu-
larly grateful to Philip Hoy and Joseph Harrison of The Waywiser
Press for their many years of support.

Dear friends—in Cleveland, Port Townsend, Seattle, and Northamp-
ton—served as first readers, and beacons of encouragement, for
much of this collection. Thanks, all.

Special thanks to Eric McHenry, who weighed in on early and late
versions of the manuscript. If a book may be known by the com-
pany it keeps, I'm glad that *The Self-Styled No-Child* is marching
into the world alongside Eric's *Odd Evening*.

Jason Whitmarsh read and reread the entire collection (plus a thou-
sand other rhymes and squibs) with immense generosity and bril-
liant good cheer. Any faults in the book are his, as I took his advice
in all matters.

For the happiness in this book, I blame Polly. For the wonder, Zia
and Ani. Thank you, thank you—now and always. I love you a lot.

Contents

Contents

"We shall no doubt have now to attack the problem from another direction."

– Sigmund Freud, *Jokes and Their Relation to the Unconscious*

"Hush little baby, sleep now I pray.
Here comes an old man to take you away."

– "Señora Santa Ana," traditional Mexican lullaby

"John Fogerty says that the old man is down the road. Is he?"

– Nicholson Baker, *The Anthologist*

Cradle Song

You're just a baby,
And as such, may be
Susceptible to lies
(And wonder, and surprise):

Left is hither,
Hither is yon,
Santa Claus has a Santa mask on;

Right is backwards,
Backwards is broken;
Baby's first words go unspoken:

You're just a dad—
Spark-lit and sad—
And I'm you, in training,
And I'm gaining.

The Art of Poetry

I need to read more poems by Kenneth Koch.
I misspoke.
What I meant to imply
(before that knife came whizzing by)
is that my life's become a dangerous joke.

Some days it seems there're ten of me, not two.
Two I can do;
I like the company.
The funny thing about poetry
is nothing, or nothing I'm privy to.

And still I conjure eight selves for applause.
There are laws:
a skinny man can't eat
his fatter kin. An indiscreet
secret, it makes us puke. Puke gives us pause.

A shelter shouldn't shelter so much rope.
If Wendy Cope
were listening—no, she's not.
This ill-got whatnot's not so hot.
It's me, ten chairs, a jacked-up gyroscope.

All hail the hangman, curse the cuffèd fool.
That's old-school;
the way out's way-out rhyme.
Not so: I'm running out of time.
The laugh's on me … it's constant, loud, and cruel.

Seasonalia

Summer
isn't Joe
McCarthy, it's Joe
Strummer.

Winter
isn't Harold
Lloyd, it's Harold
Pinter.

What I Want

Not the blustery nutsack,
not the mousy squealer,
not the cautious, chronic
even-keeler—

Not the sullen mumbler,
not the rambling bore,
not the halting cross talk from
behind the door—

Not the youngster's singsong
nor his artless slur,
not the graveside pining
of the parishioner—

A ten-part joke,
a twenty for my trouble,
a fuck for fuck's sake,
rain on this rubble

Trades I Would Make

Ronald Reagan for Donald Fagen.
Tijuana for Madonna.
This vale of tears for ten good years.
This schmuck I picked up in Indonesia for a bucket of anesthesia.
An icicle for a bicycle.
My neighbor's hollyhock trellis for Dock Ellis.
Jim (or Jimmy-o, if he'll permit) DeMint for a bit of lint.
A pay-as-you-go princess (read: overpriced hotté) for an iced
    latte.
A booster seat for some rooster meat.
A year in jail for some kale.
A turtle (either box or leatherhead) for a feather bed.
Gehrig, Unitas, Chamberlain (a bunch of dead jocks) for lunch
    with Redd Foxx.
A cat named Frisky for a vat of whiskey.
The color red for a feller named Jed.
A crate of elastic for a second-rate spastic.
A "C'mon, Cody, that's not very PC" shellacking for (and why
    not?) the Academy of American Poets' backing.
The Jackie Gleason Diet for a little peace and quiet.
Someone who dislikes (unlike us) V. for a ficus tree.
An acceptable level of risk for a bowl of lobster bisque.
Former Seattle Seahawk and current KIRO newscaster Steve
    Raible for a tucked-away-in-the-corner-and-absolutely-not-
    double-booked New Year's Eve table.
My imprisoned twin (and please, treat him nice) for Jim Rice.
A surfer-turned-robber's botched bank job ("gnarly") for Bob
    Marley.
These "Good God, I'm suddenly feeling cold and sick" shivers for
    "Mick the Quick" Rivers.
The voices in my head for Joyce's "The Dead."
A damaged and circling Space Shuttle that NASA won't let dock
    for a pet rock.
My EVIL THOUGHTS (evil; did I stammer?) for a hammer.
Electronica rap for a quick, uh, nap.

A punch in the ear for a buncha beer.

My girlfriend's personality-test result ("Freako Chick," which quite shocked her) for Ferdie Pacheco, the quick-stitch Fight Doctor.

A rotten grin for a cotton gin.

An irresponsible payout for a possible way out.

A hanging slider for a spider.

President William "Who Wants to Fight?" Howard Taft for a Million-Points-of-Light–powered raft.

Any two items of choice apparel (coats, stockings, pants) for Joyce Carol Oates's mocking glance.

Today's sorrows for tomorrow's.

Overheard speech by Shakespeare when he was drunk and distracted (minor quotes) for you-can't-really-say-that-about-Zeppelin redacted liner notes.

Some bullshit homeroom teacher no one wants for a home-run hitter who also bunts.

"Hey, choose me" pandering for some woozy meandering.

Holly round the house for a Muhammad Ali roundhouse.

A Roman brick ruin for a romantic shoo-in.

Someone mistaking me for Lance Armstrong ("Hi, Lance!") for silence.

A Fujitsu waterproof shower phone (or a dour crone) for an hour alone.

Some honest-to-God (God? You bet) belief for some debt relief.

Fred Astaire for bus fare.

My two-timin' great-uncle for Simon & Garfunkel.

A bought-in-the-Market-Square mini-drum for the bare minimum.

My favorite Yeti for Dave Righetti.

Any kind of already-banned quota for Manny Mota.

My iPhone, my Swiffer, my fogless mirror, anything that is, I swear to you, shoddy, for a "Whatever, it was hot when I brought it to you" toddy.

John Travolta, Gabe Kaplan, or Lawrence Hilton-Jacobs (really, any *Welcome Back, Kotter* entertainer) for a Bangladeshi otter trainer.

An almond steamer for a lemur.

Some long-suppressed gossip about former Baltimore Mayor Kurt (which is how he still likes to be addressed) Schmoke for your best joke.

A major-sized mystery caper for a plagiarized History paper.

The ghost of Truman for some roasted cumin.

The dropping of charges (reckless endangerment, indecent exposure) for closure.

A "Dear Twit" letter for something a bit better.

The less-than-distinguished GOP field for a DiCaprio biopic: *Leo, Revealed*.

A drawer of dimes for some more rhymes.

A veiled promise of matrimony from Mr. Met ("I do, but not yet") for a true tête-à-tête.

Bounty, the quicker picker-upper, for some no-count count's Brie-with-liquor-kicker supper.

A cup of roux for a schtup or two.

A battle-tested cry ("Let us in!") for the rest of my medicine.

A brand-new wok for Lou Brock.

An ain't-I-wild, flapper-style milieu for a childnapper who aims to steal you.

A game of catch for an aimless letch.

The bark of a seal for anything real.

Faye Dunaway for a foreign—"How you say?"—runaway.

A staggering ("Just one last swig") Billy Joel for a big chili bowl.

A "Baby baby what's the matter?" kiss for that or this.

My ex-girlfriend (a pill-popper, a lout, a jaw-clencher) for a kill-or-be-killed proper outlaw adventure.

These constant cries of "Why, God?" for a colossal-sized tripod.

Anyone from the rougher parts of Paris for anyone dumb enough to spare us.

Some this-is-so-good-you-must've-made-it-in-culinary-school chocolate for a multi-tool player who'll walk a lot.

A tipsy poodle for some dipsy-doodle.
Any ridiculous status (executive! platinum! wined and dined!
    preferred!) for a kind word.
The straight and narrow for a great sombrero.

This Is the Neighbor Kid Who Killed the Cat

This is the neighbor kid who killed the cat.
This is your father who thinks like that.
This is your mother who throws up her hands.
This is the algorithm that misunderstands.

This is the jackhammer that hates the rock.
This is the safety at war with the Glock.
This is your lab partner, stockpiling Xanax.
This is your captain—watch as he panics.

This is your nightmare, bright as day.
This is your police scanner. What will it say?
These are your boots to wipe on the mat.
Mark down your casualties. Hang up your hat.

Haiku

I'm a mountain and
you're a new weather pattern
that crushes mountains.

Quatrains

Rotgut makes me merry, pornos leave me limp;
I chatted with my uncle (my uncle is a chimp);
"You ought to move to Switzerland" (that's what my uncle said);
"The only known survivors will be swimming in your head."

I didn't move to Switzerland; instead, I bought a car;
I filled the tank with vinegar and didn't get very far.
Some chimps live in treetops, some chimps carry knives;
My uncle is an expert on Botticelli's wives.

"You ought to move to Timbuktu" (that's what the tea leaves said);
"The only known survivors will be sleeping in your bed."
So I went to northern Mali where I met an undertaker
Who specialized in overheads. I found it hard to shake her.

Chimps are just a metaphor (for what, I couldn't say);
A poem is a container that keeps the ghosts away;
Sandro never married (the prospect gave him nightmares);
My uncle is in prison for manipulating flight fares.

I'd offer you some rotgut, but I don't have any more.
The only known survivors are waiting by the door.
I'd offer you a porno, but really, what's the use.
Everything's been neutralized. The games all end in deuce.

When Addison Strode the Earth

for Addison Lansdell

When Addison strode the earth,
Pterodactyls flew breezily, breezily overhead.

When Addison strode the earth,
Glaciers calved and lo, the plates tectonicked.

When Addison strode the earth,
Vesuvius covered its mouth, oblivious.

When Addison strode the earth,
Erasmus was laughing, Shakespeare was musing, the Russians
    were coming, the dollar was falling—
Just so, just yesterday,
When Addison strode the earth.

My Uncle, in Hephzibah, Georgia, Rises from the Dead and Writes a Double Clerihew

Osama Bin Laden
Ain' no mode'n
Man. He a throwback.
He go yack-yack.

Osama Bin Laden
Be'n fo'godden.
We gah In'e'net, nine'y-inch Tee-vee.
He in the sea.

Mind of Winter

I'd like to write some lines about the snow,
but—I dunno,
the snow seems so
fleeting:
a flock of gulls, late for a meeting.

Forgoing snow, I fix upon the wind—
and look! it's pinned
a suitably chagrined
old fop
against the doors of a Stop & Shop.

A pill might help—or coffee refill, stat—
some way to combat
the inkling that
these days
are laced with malice and malaise.

I stumbled ere I fell—a tired turn.
If Stevens, stern
as he was, could learn
to chill
when nothing went his way, there's hope, still.

Small Suite

Heartbeat, Eleven Weeks

Our child! Our striver!
Our little keep-aliver …

***

Third Trimester

Dusk; inscrutable sky. A kid high-fives
a Honda
antenna.
The near end, Love, of our practice-run lives.

***

Origin Song

for Zia Rosenwaike Walker

Littlest Walker, can't even crawl—
Cost us a shilling at the shopping mall—
Came with a rattle, came with a shake—
Banana espresso—wide awake …

Stashed in a treetop, fashioned to fall—
Summons the cops with a pelican call—
Sunlight's a goner, moon's on the make—
Mistakes our Zia for Veronica Lake …

***

Staggering Backwards,

my daughter fell;
I caught her. Still,

I couldn't speak with my wife,
couldn't walk back the what-if;

and for what was left of the day,
I felt bereft and wanted to die.

***

In Two Hundred Years

Zia
will be a
what?
     Awful thought:
we've wrought
a time bomb; a gust of wind; an eventual no-see-um.
Carpe diem.

Appetite

Marvin wasn't starvin'—but he was hungry, so he decided to hunt down a hog. Little Marvin! Eight years old! In exurbia! It would be funny if it wasn't so terrible.

You read the many stories about Marvin's father's gun; about the five-year-old at the park; about the babysitter. You're a grown-up and you have your opinions. But I want to suggest that there may be another life beyond the one that we're living!

In a thousand years, Marvin and I will be about the same age. We live in the same age, now. You say, Stop it, there's no Marvin, this is a story, your story. Tell that to Marvin, in his tiny, Marvin-sized cell.

A Skeleton Walks Into a Bar

All the death chatter, the gloomy
back and forth:
for what it's worth,
it's beginning to get to me.

So the skeleton orders an Orgasm
and someone snickers …
but they're all cocksuckers!!
(for "bar," read "skull-yard," *passim*).

The scene ends with a pileup
atop our protagonist:
a punch-drunk fabulist
pops in and claps for a mop

and—fuck it, it's just a joke.
Meanwhile, move
closer, Love,
now that we're both awake.

Disconsolation

Intimacy,
you see,
is our grail.
It's where we fail.

We grab any chance
to advance
our status—
because a dark god shat us.

We'd kill everything
to bring
on silence we'd mishear as prayer.
There there.

Deuteronomy, Continued

The wolf shall overtake thee and devour thee; and the parts that remain shall be devoured a second time; and the wolf shall not be slaked.

The worst that thou know shall become as the best; and the best that thou know shall become as the worst; and the difference shall not be felt; and thy questions and cries shall go unanswered.

The LORD shall tickle thee with a feather duster, and boot thee with a tire iron, and goose thee with an actual goose.

And pestilence shall rain; and frogs shall multiply; and the best ointment shall avail thee not.

And thy skin shall become like the bark of a tree; but rougher, let's say: a thousand times rougher.

The LORD shall smite thee with a mighty upward blow, and thy head shall pop upward, much as the head of the Rock 'Em Sock 'Em Robot, many millennia hence.

Thou shalt go to the zoo and punch a monkey. And the monkey shall punch thee back and the zookeeper shall take the monkey away.

Un-jokes

1

Andrei Codrescu
couldn't rescue
a gnat from a firing squad.
(Or wouldn't. "Izz just a *gnat*," he'd say. No: it's a creature of God.)

2

After Years of Battling Van Gogh

Picasso
put up his hands and cried, "No más!" So
he retired to a yurt to read the Koran.
(Wrong, on every count, including the yurt. And it was Roberto
    Durán.)

A Mad Gardener's Half Dozen

He thought he saw a Hula-Hoop
    As big as twenty suns:
He looked again, and found it was
    An octopus, with guns.
"I mean no harm, my well-armed friend,"
    He said—that Prince of Puns.

He thought he saw a Telescope
    That held the Evening Sky:
He looked again, and found it was
    A Dear John Letter (sigh).
"My name is Jim; it's not for me!"
    He said—a Valiant Try.

He thought he saw a Garbage Truck
    Upended in a ditch:
He looked again, and found it was
    A naked, taunting Witch.
"My manhood she's misprized," he said;
    "It lifts without a hitch!"

He thought he saw a Cup of Milk
    All Curdled in the Heat:
He looked again, and found it was
    A Bluesman's Outsized Feet.
"I like to kick it some myself,"
    He said—just off the beat.

He thought he saw a Prison Guard
    Who wore Chantilly Lace:
He looked again, and found it was
    A Booty Call, from Grace.
"I'm tied up till the 3rd," he said,
    "But text me, just in case."

He thought he saw a Poltergeist
    That cut a movie queue:
He looked again, and found it was
    The End of Me and You.
"Perhaps you'll meet again," he said,
    "In jail, or Kathmandu."

He thought he saw a Suicide
    Beneath the Shaded Elm:
He looked again, and found it was
    A Captain at his Helm.
"The whitecaps on the rocks," he said—
    "They tend to overwhelm."

Upward Mobility

From Troma to the MOMA,
From Britney to the Whitney,
From pork 'n' beans to aubergines,
From delicatessens to French lessons;

From Dr. Phil to Gwen Ifill,
From Jim Belushi to albacore sushi,
From Jacqueline Susann to coq au vin,
From "out of my store, man" to tipping the doorman;

From baloney to Antonioni,
From darts to a Master of Arts,
From us in tears to me in three years,
From Styrofoam cups to green technology start-ups.

Revision

"At a health spa in China, an eel swam up a man's penis."
– *Harper's*, November 2011

I don't mind eels.
Except as meals.
And when they swim up my penis.

I Know, I Know,

live and let live—
but I give
Ann Romney a
sleeping pill
and she *still*
complains, Love,
of
insomnia!
I miss the old days: Max's
Kansas City,
CBGB—
but now everything's shitty,
everything's a worthless freebie.
The gun murderers, just to be safe, also bring axes,
and Mitt Romney, our resident
dunce,
wants
to be president.

2011–2012: A Romnibus

If I Ever Say, Even in My Sleep,

Mitt Romney,
he da bomb, knee
me in the nuts.
Slit
my gullet.
Murder me with paper cuts.

***

Mitt Romney and Anthony Comstock: The Rom Com

They meet cute, at the post office.
Later, a dinner (the rice pilaf is
delicious, as is the roast goat)
and a quiet evening of book burning.
No temple garments are shed. Note,
though, the hard stares, the terrible yearning.

***

Vice-Squad Clerihew

Marco Rubio
is the second coming of boxer/murderer/Havana-vacationer Jack
    ("Sparky"—his boxing nickname, yo) Ruby! Oh,
and Romney's Oswald.
Oh, and the Secret Service just called.

***

The Romney Doctrine (Found Poem)

"I'm not
familiar precisely
with exactly
what I said,
but I stand by what
I said,
what-
ever it was."

***

Voting Booth Drama

Paul Ryan's cowlick
doesn't care how sick
you might become—
and it's mum
on how to pay
for your long hospital stay.
Now quick,
answer this (by pulling the appropriate lever):
Will you be 42 forever?
(*Forever*, sayeth the cowlick.)

***

Two Limericks

In a rich guy's McMansion in Boca,
The warrior Romney-o spoke-a:
"They're *entitled*," he sneered
(The whole thing was weird),
And half of the country awoke-a.

With six weeks to go, Barry blinks—
And Romney's back in it! (Fox thinks);
"But unless Mitt can pick up
Ohio, this hiccup
Means nothing" (our strategist winks).

***

The Last Words We'll Ever Write About Romney

Mittmentum
sent 'im
(almost)
to DC.
He lost,
which is fit. Go easy.

News That Stays News

So I was talking to my friend Lester
about the sequester.
Lester's wife Esther
was lost in a nor'wester,
after leaving Lester
for a clergyman-turned-carny who guessed her
weight and then "blessed" her
and caressed her and undressed her.
"A molester,"
fumed Lester.
Lester feels everything's beginning to fester.
I asked what his students were reading this semester;
he said, "I don't know: *Infinite Jest* or
You Too Can Drum Like Pete Best or

what is this a test or
something?" I tried to steer us back to the sequester,
but then in walked Lester's sister, Hester.
Hester's an investor
in the West Chester
Poetry Center's Electromagnetic Double-Sonnet Tester,
so I said, "Hey, Hester,
I hate to pester
you but do you think you could run that Tester
over my poem featuring Lester
and the sequester
and, God rest her soul, Esther?"
Later, Hester pressed up against me on her best, or
second-best, sofa bed. Please don't tell Lester.

"More Than Half of America's Experiencing Moderate to Extreme Doubt"

– Heard on Michigan Radio, July 18, 2012, 9:58 a.m.

A: What? That can't be right, can it?

B: There's no fucking way that's right.

We Hated Our Lives

We hated our lives so we dug up the fern
And gassed the azaleas and emptied the urn

And severed our fingers and salted our toes
Which caused us to stumble, but that's how it goes

We jetted to India, jetted to Spain
We scattered our clothes in the wind and the rain

We gobbled the photos and drank all the ink
And tortured a Gabonese charlatan shrink

And who would be waiting, upon our return?
Our kids, at our doorstep, expressing concern

Poem with an Epigraph from *Edward Lear, King of Nonsense,* a Biography for Young People

"Now he felt truly alone!"

This old man! He lived in San Remo!
And listened to nothing but emo!
His cat Foss was dead!
Of cancer, it's said!
Since nobody'd yet thought of chemo!

One, Two

1

Polly in the sunlight, Polly in the shade,
Polly on a battered boat, Polly in a glade

Polly stealing pumpkins, Polly on the run,
Polly with a checkered past, Polly with a gun

Polly with some holly, Polly in a funk,
Polly with a troubadour, singing to a monk

Polly O Great Golly, Polly Fucking Christ,
Polly with that gun again, planning for a heist

2

I like your voice at four a.m.—
the soft edges, the submarine low notes.
I like your body's edges, too—
recalled, in the evening, as we remove our coats.

Conditional

If worker bees would work for free,
We'd chance a honeymoon;
And you'd let go that thing I said
Yesterday afternoon.

The sun would quickstep in the sky,
March would yield to June,
And you'd let go that thing I said
Yesterday afternoon.

The Jerk Speaks

So this knob, this Santa, is all "Can you help a brother out," all "I'll make it worth your while"—and I'm thinking *lump sum,* I mean, I seen the work order, but we're like *flying*—five hours, we're done— and he's all "No, it's hourly," and I'm like "Like hell it's hourly," and somebody gets up into somebody and I ain't saying nothing more till I talk to that lady on that subway sign who's maybe I think a lawyer.

Days, Months, Years

They come with more speed.
It's nothing we need:
a text, a news feed—
maybe a baby:
next, next.
The 401(k)s, the paid-off houses—
someone grouses
that his grave's
too near the freeway.
The baby waves
so long. So little leeway.

Petronius

The Arbiter of Elegance would sit us
Around a tray of pig and *sciacchetrà*. His aim:
Pleasure; his method: pass the cup.
He thought it a science. Thus, writes Tacitus,
"He idled into fame."

Success at court, and then … rumors about
A rival. Charges came, from jealous Tigellinus—
Dabbler, historical hiccup.
We should have carved that man with a hook, but
We didn't have it in us.

Nobody lives forever. Well, long odds.
Slit your wrists; talk poetry—so the day might go.
It was like everyone gave up:
The artist Nero; then most of the gods.
It happened years ago.

A Long Time Ago, in Italy

A Portuguese sot, pumped up with Madeira,
Paid seventy-thousand lire
To schtup a cup of oxtail stew.
Distasteful, but true.

Mid-January

Season of satire, says Northrop Frye.
See the pine trees, needling the sky.

Aurora Blackout

Some shadow version of James Holmes
roams
free—
which, according to Senator Ron Johnson, Republican of
   Wisconsin, is how it should be.*

* "'The fact of the matter is, there are magazines, 30-round magazines, that are just common all over the place, and you simply can't keep these weapons out of the hands of sick, demented individuals that want to do harm,' Mr. Johnson said on 'Fox News Sunday.' 'And when you try and do it, you restrict our freedoms.'" – *The New York Times*, July 23, 2012

OK, a Dude's Dead, But You Can Go

It looked like a gang sign—
and I work hard for what's mine.

I hate to involve her,
but it was my grandma's revolver.

I shot, like, one round.
(I was standing my ground.)

Three, Briefly

Audible Acceleration

My man Wystan
was a piston!
(A piston, yo,
makes the engine go.)

***

Amy Clampitt, Wary Huntress

would pillage
(for blessèd art)
the dictionary
in the very
heart
of the West Village.

***

At a Tennis Court, at Amherst College, Near the Frost Library

What a letdown:
they've taken the net down.

Autobiography

It's 1966, and

Colonel Sanders
meanders
toward my mom. She's got a couple of closets that are, say, walk-ins,
and she kind of head-gestures to the Colonel—wait, no, that was
    Jay Hawkins.

***

Me

I'm a stand of English ivy: uproot me.
I'm a broken donkey: shoot me.

My tea leaves make shitty tea.
I'm growing older: pity me.

***

"How Beautiful It Is to Do Nothing, and Then Rest Afterward"

— Spanish proverb

Sleep is a kind of blind bliss.
It's how we practice
for the succeeding century,
the one we won't see.

Most Beautiful and Most Wonderful

God says Yes—
The Devil says No—
Darwin shrugs, says Take it slow—

God says Today—
The Devil says Tomorrow—
Darwin maps out a million years of sorrow—

A million years of sorrow—
And grandeur, too—
Ga-ga-ga-ga-ga, ga-ga-ga-goo—

God says Wake—
The Devil starts to snore—
Darwin sidles out the side-back door—

All the Splendid Babies

are agog in Prague—
but for
yours:
She's in a lobby in Abu Dhabi.

Pronunciation Lessons

1

P. G. Wodehouse
misunderstood *Maus*
when he read it from the grave.
"The mice are bloody off their onion. At least the cats behave."

2 (Couched in a Riddle)

Laura Nyro
ate a gyro
and then, much later, died of ovarian cancer.
(This riddle has no answer.)

Lenox, Early Spring

The large black birds stay largely out of sight.
Squirrels scurry; the wind does what the wind does;
and Amy Clampitt's ghost shudders, because
it's six o'clock, and cold, and almost night.

My next-door neighbor switches on a light,
which turns her to shadow behind the gauze
curtains, until—some cause, and she withdraws.
For thirty years I haven't felt quite right.

I love the shots of Amy caught in bliss.
I love the hemlocked hills, the crests of snow,
the looming library, the quiet graves.
I'm not afraid—so far—of death: it waves
its tiny fist: I follow; I let go.
But look: the sky's aglow. There's that. There's this.

This Again

"Whisper, whisper," whisper the devils,
But you've learned now not to reply.

Their only lesson—*it all unravels*—
Is a wearisome, not-quite lie.

Six Lines

You can't rhyme
time:
time's its own thing.
Like death.
Hold your breath,
see what that'll bring.

Absolut Power Corrupts Absolut-ly

I like Andy Kaufman—not the wrestling stuff so much—but some
    of the stand-up—and on *Taxi*, of course, as Latka—
but what I really like is vodka.

The Garden

He thought he saw a Cancer Cell
    Divide itself in Two:
He looked again, and found it was
    A note from Vida Blue.
"You can't go back in time," it read.
    So brief. So sad. So true.

He thought he saw the Singing Moon
    Reflected on the Water:
He looked again, and found it was
    His eighteen-month-old Daughter.
"I'm not sure she can swim," he said;
    "Perhaps a Druid taught her."

He thought he saw a Charleston Church
    Exploding in the night:
He looked again, and found it was
    Just that, in black and white.
"A coward's at the wheel," he said,
    And held his children tight.

Litany (Unfinished)

It's afternoon; the restaurant starts to clear.
An ad for Afro Sheen,
then Borax. Forks appear
on tabletops. It's useless; strike the scene.

When Blake felt close to death, he sang of heaven.
He died at six p.m.,
a Sunday, and someone
should sing that song today, ad infinitum.

Newtown Carol

I went to bed, everyone was dying or already dead
I went to bed, everyone was dying or already dead
Some of this dying happened, some was in my head

The dying on the outside was impossible to reverse
The dying on the outside was impossible to reverse
The dying on the inside was a blessing and a curse

For blessing just say cowardice, part of me won't mind
For blessing just say cowardice, part of me won't mind
A curse because the true dead left all these songs behind

The Self-Styled No-Child

The self-styled No-Child
sets his fedora by the Menorah.

He reads the evening papers by tapers.
He washes his galoshes.

And when a chill sets in, he strokes his chin,
imagines sleep, and wonders if the fire will keep.

And when his own child cries, he tries
to chime away all Time with nursery rhyme.

NOTES

A MAD GARDENER'S HALF DOZEN: The nine stanzas that comprise Lewis Carroll's "The Mad Gardener's Song" appear fitfully in *Sylvie and Bruno* (1889) and *Sylvie and Bruno Concluded* (1893).

POEM WITH AN EPIGRAPH FROM *EDWARD LEAR, KING OF NONSENSE*, A BIOGRAPHY FOR YOUNG PEOPLE: This charming biography, written by Gloria Kamen, was published by Atheneum in 1990. It's now out of print.

PETRONIUS: Petronius's suicide of 66 A.D. is described in the 16th and final book of Tacitus's *Annals* (translated by Alfred John Church and William Jackson Brodribb): "Yet he did not fling away life with precipitate haste, but having made an incision in his veins and then, according to his humor, bound them up, he again opened them, while he conversed with his friends…. And he listened to them as they repeated, not thoughts on the immortality of the soul or on the theories of philosophers, but light poetry and playful verses."

MID-JANUARY: For more (much more) on Northrop Frye's pairings of the archetypal literary forms and the seasons, see the third essay in *The Anatomy of Criticism: Four Essays* (1957).

AURORA BLACKOUT: James Holmes murdered twelve people at a movie theater in Aurora, Colorado, in 2012.

LITANY (UNFINISHED): For a fuller account of William Blake's death (including his words to his wife: "Stay, Kate! Keep just as you are—I will draw your portrait—for you have ever been an angel to me"), see Peter Ackroyd's *Blake: A Biography* (1996).

A Note About the Author

Photograph: © Polly Rosenwaike, 2015

Cody Walker is the author of *Shuffle and Breakdown* (Waywiser Press, 2008) and the co-editor of *Alive at the Center: Contemporary Poems from the Pacific Northwest* (Ooligan Press, 2013). His poems have appeared in *The Yale Review, Parnassus, Slate, Poetry Northwest, The Hecht Prize Anthology*, and *The Best American Poetry* (2007 and 2015); his essays have appeared online in *The New Yorker* and *The Kenyon Review*. He lives with his family in Ann Arbor, where he teaches English at the University of Michigan.

Other Books from Waywiser

Other Books from Waywiser

Bradford Gray Telford, *Perfect Hurt*
Matthew Thorburn, *This Time Tomorrow*
Cody Walker, *Shuffle and Breakdown*
Deborah Warren, *The Size of Happiness*
Clive Watkins, *Already the Flames*
Clive Watkins, *Jigsaw*
Richard Wilbur, *Anterooms*
Richard Wilbur, *Mayflies*
Richard Wilbur, *Collected Poems 1943-2004*
Norman Williams, *One Unblinking Eye*
Greg Williamson, *A Most Marvelous Piece of Luck*
Greg Williamson, *The Hole Story of Kirby the Sneak and Arlo the True*

FICTION
Gregory Heath, *The Entire Animal*
Mary Elizabeth Pope, *Divining Venus*
K. M. Ross, *The Blinding Walk*
Gabriel Roth, *The Unknowns**
Matthew Yorke, *Chancing It*

ILLUSTRATED
Nicholas Garland, *I wish ...*
Eric McHenry and Nicholas Garland, *Mommy Daddy Evan Sage*
Greg Williamson, *The Hole Story of Kirby the Sneak and Arlo the True*

NON-FICTION
Neil Berry, *Articles of Faith: The Story of British Intellectual Journalism*
Mark Ford, *A Driftwood Altar: Essays and Reviews*
Richard Wollheim, *Germs: A Memoir of Childhood*

* Co-published with Picador